CHRISTMAS CANTICLES

ADELE SERONDE

CHRISTMAS CANTICLES

ISBN: 978-0-578-42995-3
Pegasus Publishing

Published by Adele Seronde
Sedona, Arizona

Cover: Oil Painting "Fire Wheel" by Adele Seronde
Cover and book design by Jane Perini

DEDICATED TO ALL
PEOPLE EVERYWHERE:

Please accept these few hopeful wishes for this
time of loving. It is a moment for reaching out
to each other, for admiring the living creatures
of the Earth, animals, birds, plants, insects, even
the rocks and waters and sky.

It is our time to rededicate ourselves to protecting
and nurturing each other and our earth itself. It is
a season for turning money and power into energy
of love, for using all our natural energies to create
newly charged lives, exciting experiments and
lasting solutions.

Even for short moments and short lives, flowers
give such fragrance, color and beauty, they unite
the whole world.

Be as flowers!

As God's star shines
we are reborn as Light
    in dark stables
        of our hearts.

Christmas rekindles
    new Christ Child
        within us
    His holy Light returns.

As wild world wars,
Christ Jesus smiles
with his mother,
and sleeps in Love's arms.

Animals, close by, bathe His being
    with warmth of their breathing
    in his smile
Oxen, donkeys, cows,
    shepherd's sheep and goats
take on His haloes
    with grace.

Kings of freedom
        they come,
enthroned in scarlet,
        crowned in gold,
            bearing gifts.

Riding high in camels,
bedecked in splendor,
they bring their love
        to this Child.

Three gifts of wisdom
come with the kings:
frankincense
as Spirit, gold as Light,
and myrrh of Rebirth.
They come to welcome him,
Jesus-Christ Child,
home at last.

Gather up
our wishes and dreams.
Hang them high
as
our candles of light.

We are live ornaments
hung on God's tree
as prayers
for life's wisdom.

Under God's tree:
   our offerings
      and His
innocence,
courage,
delight.

See!
Each ornament, a life,
        is unique!
Filled with color
        they dance free!

Each life a statement
        of love—or denial,
a yearning to love,
        rounded in grace
                and able to give.

Green is heart-chakra's color:
oxygen to Earth.
Are we emeralds?
Will our hearts
become green in your grace,
dear God?
How can we know what you give?

Have you held hummingbird's heart
    in your hands?
Nestled feathers of fear?
    No?
Its heart is magnet
    for all mankind's heart
    as it struggles to live
    now.

It flew into my house of despair
            by mistake—
could only escape
            too
if I shared its fear!
God, deliver us both
            to your Love—
                    set us free!

            God hears hermit-thrush
                    flute calls
                            at dusk.
            We, who listen for Light,
                    will too.

Christ's blessed are women
who hold refugee children, dreams, loves
in their arms.

To hold each life close
as beloved child is
Earth-Mother's gift in us.

Women have ultimate challenge
            today!
Make justice move
        to God's hand!
God's wisdom
                lives
in women's intuitive
        wish to create
                beauty—
                    now—
as a catalyst
                    to enhance
                    equal justice for all
                    live beings.

Big cities can be manipulated
by politicians
and greed!
but

women choose more often
to protect children,
and all beings
in need.

Kaleidoscope city lights
        as seen from God's plane:
        brilliant echoes of
                    hope!

Some cities still dazzle
        with iridescent wings
            summer festivals
children's swings and murals.
        Others rust away:
their subways flooded
            by storm,
their power grids browning out,
        their poverty entrapping
            all last hope
                but
        for a glimmer
            of Christmas lights--
a brief remembrance
        of
Love's beauty.

Grass spears
        pierce
asphalted sidewalks
        of heart,
eclipse dark alleys
        of hurt.
Grass sings in wind's chalice
            of sound;
        its song penetrates
        our heart's cement!

Every city street holds challenges
how bring light?
Children's smiles, flowers
feel right!

Tonight....
Christ is born again Whole
in all living creatures
of our world.
Come fill my memory with surprises!
Meadowlark wing-flash
of love!

Flowers of wild beauty
            are hung
      on life's tree
as candles
of sun-lit praise.
            Swallows go.
Bats take their places
      in dusk's minuet
            of sky diving!

            Hear crickets dissemble
                  winter's coming
                  play roulette
                  with outgoing joy!

Jesus plays with my mind.
   "Be a child!" He says.
   "That is Love's sacred joy!"

      We are
   all wild children
         lost
   in dying world's heart.
   How can we reach you?

"Just sing me truth
        in all your songs
        of your life,"
says our Lord
            to each child.

Ride in dream's arms
on soft wings
of desire
urging you to fly
with joy.

Do our children
      have a future?
            Do we care?
Leave a legacy of love?
Can beauty deliver them
            into hope?
            Running horses?
            Flying swans?
Whole world of flying
      and holding its arms out
            to catch
universal stars?

"Are these children
        all mine?"
asks each human being.
"Each one and all,"
        says Christ.
Not in nameless future:
        the second coming of Christ—
                but here and Now!

All children
surrounded by sea
need growing:
two ultimate poles
        of existence.
Square and circle,
        black and white,
all shades of color
                of truth—
        and dark holes.
        Yin and Yang:
Matriarch of living,
        Father-God of life.
        Earth-child,
striving up to sky's Light
down to soil's embrace
        reaches
        God's love.

We are dumbed
by decibels of noise
          so static
    that heart cannot sing!
Wild truth is clarion-call of heart
          who will hear?
White apple tree blossoms
still sing!

Electronic drown-out
          carries reason
              away.
All our values too.
          How
    do we choose
    what to keep?
    TURN IT OFF!
Listen to silence
          of sound!

Computerized strivations
       of mind-search
  sing singularity's
     high song,
        but
at nano point striving
     for Nirvana,
            they need
        God's prayer smile.

God's central Being
    lives everywhere;
in far internet vision
      as well.

Swallows, robins and nightingales,
horses, foxes and wolves
live again
in our dying Earth's womb.
Arachnes, butterflies, snakes
feel His light too—
we are resurrected Nature
crying out to bloom—
as poems of love.

Swift movement
of spirit
stirs my blood
like dolphin dive,
owl wing
of Light.

When our Christmas tree
        was taken down,
Its balsam-fir needles
            still
        smelled sweet.
Made into pillows
            of
        fragrant love,
        its needles
            could heal
shriveled hearts.

Love's solar panels
            trap
        radiant light
              in
mind chamber,
ignite heart.

Can we open
        our soil-veins
when Love sprinkles
        rain's fragrance
              on our Earth?

Are we cleaved by white light?
        In depths of sky?
        do our colors emerge?
Wisdom's color a mind-feast
                new facet of love:
dragon-eyed rainbow!

Love in action:
        learns aspired wisdom
                of heart
lives to find truth in each smile.

When we eat of Light's wisdom
colors shine in our eyes
as full rainbows!

We are carrots, lentils, potatoes
of God's wisdom menu

of foods.
Artichoke's God-heart center
is protected
by Love's wise living leaves.

Vegetables call to sun
        saying
"As roots of life
        we must grow!"
Our arrows of purpose
bring green promise:
        rain water
        leaf-compost
                love.

Who
replies to immigrants
        now?
        Anyone? A
rising American voice
        is crying
                "Me!
I now remember
we all were once immigrants
        too!"

        We are still
                a nation
        cleaved through
        with dissension
                but
        we now
                feel hope.

Our statue of Liberty
    still stands
with God's hand
    on the torch
        held high!

For us to move
        forward
    from here,
learn to listen
        and hear
    other's voice
    is to know
we must change:
    find ways
        to help,
and laugh at ourselves
        again.

How do we change
         mistrust
                  to
         respect?
Do we search
for small ways
         to share?
Do we offer a willing hand,
         brush away fear,
                  and
         smile as a friend?

Jesus reborn in America
this Christmas
means
truth must be
faced:
we
are all neighbors.
What *I* do now to like *you*,
can change
the world's heart.

Wherever we now live
we still have
skies,
and waters
of our land
in common
with people of all nations,
religions, races,
and dreams.

If we hang prayers
for forgiveness
on Your tree,
will You respond?

"Bring broken promises
    into my arms
and all creatures too!"
    said Jesus,
    "because
        if
I can heal ruptures,
    I can mend
    Broken people
        as well."

What is compassion
    if not hope?
        Listening,
        longing
to understand?

Moving shapes
of spring insects
        arrive too:
grasshoppers, ants, flies
        and bees.

Even lost in strange cities
        if visitors can find
            green
they feel WELCOME!

Our Earth,
planet of blue and green dreams,
is at risk.
Allow us to care!
Water Earth; it is thirsty.
Nourish our soil.
Neither poison nor pollute.
Feel its beauty
in our minds and hearts.
Grow its nutrient core
in green love.

Grow in emerald embrace
of Love's leaves.
Become a Sequoia's
huge hope.

Beauty
expands truth in mind
and hands
as
double-striated rainbow!

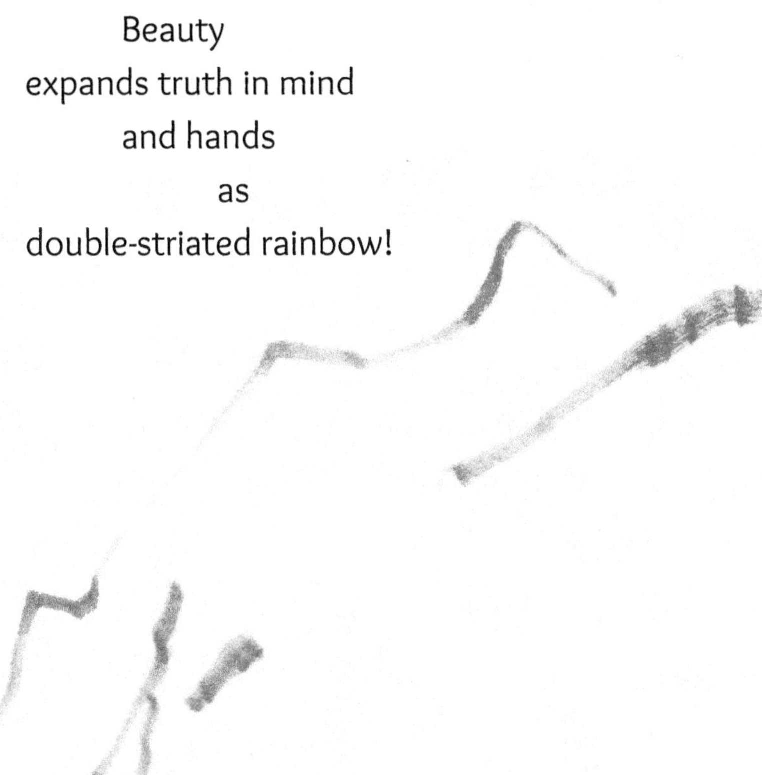

How will we know
         each truth
of movement
is a moment
         an action
                  of Grace?

Truth has many forms:
         integrity,
         courage,
         surprise!
Each claims our whole heart.

When truth prayers
hang
on our tree
all life is singing
God's song of Light.

Fragments of discarded human hearts
     fill our days—
     fill our nights—
empty our lives.
How to reassemble our souls?
Bring together bright tesserae
     of dreams
and recreate hope
as a high quantum energy
     mosaic of love.

Christ-Consciousness
        shapes
mosaics of truth:
    honesty
    freedom
and prayer.

Our new mosaic tesserae
of rainbows
form unity of hope
allows
America to forgive,
speak again with truth,
and to pray.

Can I listen again
    to life's birdsong,
    hum of insects,
    wolves howling?
    Hear
Love's canticle's song:
    Heart-breath
of all God's wilderness
in my arms?

Poems can be shortcuts
to truth:
a quiet word
instead of shouting prose rant.

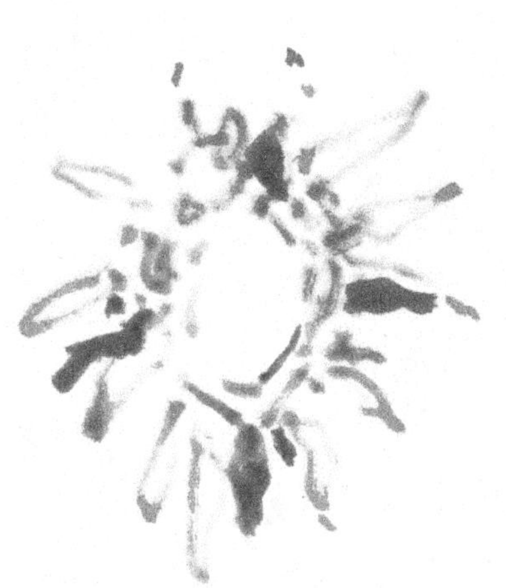

We are syllables
of word-song
strung
on His tree of Light's
necklaces.

Light is Word:
candle-fire in mind.
    When will we see
        Heaven
    on our tree?